INCREDIBLE EARTH!

Eye-opening Photos of

Our Powerful Planet

playBac
PUBLISHING

More.Brain.Power

Incredible Earth! Nature is truly as ferocious as it is magnificent.

This book offers us a unique opportunity to take a thrilling photographic journey around the world. We will dive deep into dark oceans; fly over beautiful yet dangerous lakes; stand in awe of landscapes that appear more alien than familiar; marvel at miraculous sculptures created in rock, ice, sand, and salt; and peer into volcanic craters that bubble like witches' cauldrons!

These striking and completely unaltered photographs invite us to discover the world around us in new and exciting ways: up close and in extraordinary detail.

Turn the page to discover a world that is as fantastic as it is fascinating!

The Amboseli Reserve, a haven of peace in the savanna. In Kenya, the Amboseli Reserve shelters a number of exceptional animals. The snowmelt from Mount Kilimanjaro creates marshes, which attract birds and large mammals. Among them, elephants find the vegetation and water they need to survive. They love to splash for hours surrounded by cattle egrets, so named because they peck at parasites on the backs of large animals, including cows and elephants.

A volcano that actually cooled things down!

In 1991, the Philippine volcano, Mount Pinatubo, reawakened after centuries of inactivity. At the height of its eruption an eleven-mile-wide column of cinders and glowing gases rose over eighteen miles above the crater, plunging the region into darkness and covering the landscape in ash. The volcanic dust spread throughout the planet's atmosphere, blocking some of the sun's rays and leading to a slight cooling of the entire Earth's climate that year.

PHILIPPINES, ASIA

The baobab, master of the savanna.

Despite growing in the almost desert-like savanna, the baobab tree can reach a height of ninety-eight feet, with a trunk up to thirty-nine feet in diameter. Like a sponge, the baobab soaks up water during the rainy season, which it then stores for the long dry periods common in the savanna. Due to its toughness, the baobab can live for hundreds of years! It is found in Africa and Australia.

MADAGASCAR, AFRICA

A clash of fire and water!

The islands of Hawaii have several active volcanoes, including the Kilauea Volcano, whose Pu'u 'O'o vent has poured out lava flows on the Big Island for two decades. The temperature of these glowing red rivers is more than 1,800 degrees Fahrenheit! After running underground, the scorching hot lava resurfaces and flows into the sea in a great explosion of steam, producing a magnificent spectacle! When it cools, the lava hardens and accumulates, which extends the surface of the island.

UNITED STATES, NORTH AMERICA

This rock in the Green River Gorge looks like it's floating on water.

Don't be fooled: This is not a big island, but the tip of a rock that the river has slowly eroded. Over millions of years, the Green River and its tributaries have cut into the sandstone that is found in the arid (dry) areas where the river flows. The constantly moving water has caused the river to form winding paths, called meanders. And in this picture, the winding has gotten so extreme that the river has actually formed an amazing ring of water!

UNITED STATES,
NORTH AMERICA

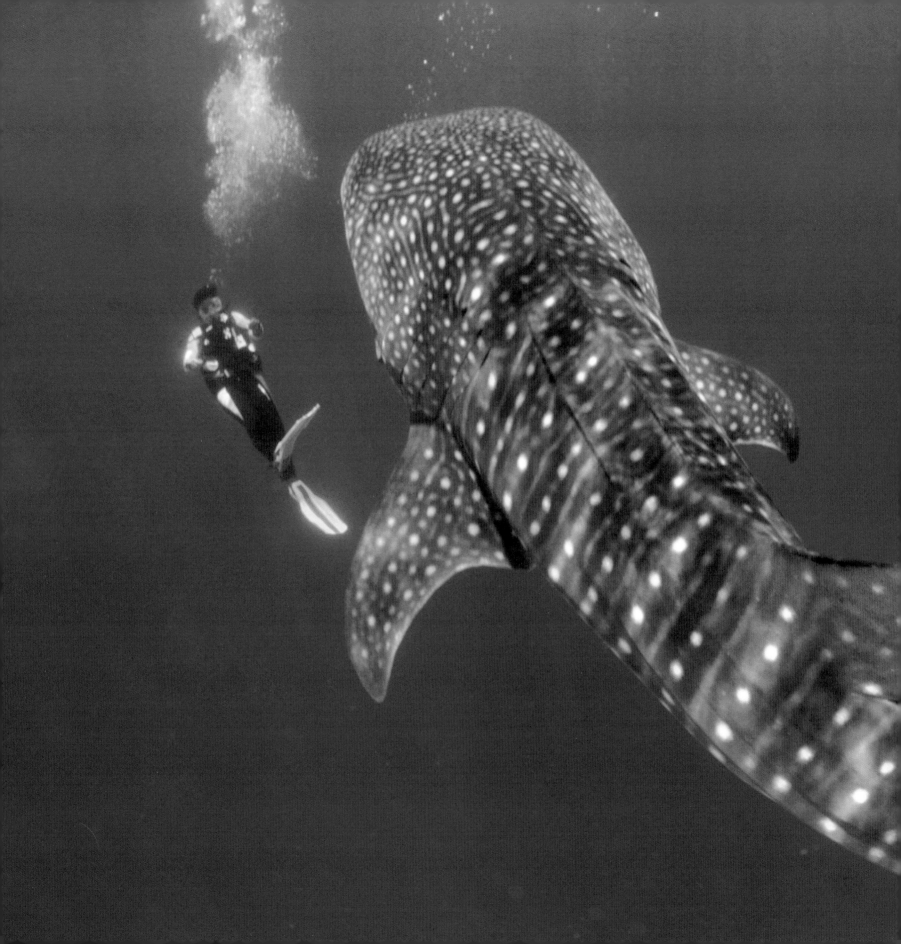

The whale shark—the biggest, but least dangerous, of the sharks!

The whale shark has the tail of a whale and the body shape of a shark. Its immense length (up to forty feet long!) makes it the biggest fish in the world. Its mouth alone can be up to five feet wide with as many as three thousand teeth. If the diver seems a little *too* calm, it is because the whale shark only eats plankton and small fish—not humans! The whale shark doesn't eat with its teeth like humans, but sucks in a mouthful of water, closes its mouth, and shoots out the water through its gills (keeping all the tasty plankton inside).

PHILIPPINES, ASIA

In Bolivia, ice "grows" in the middle of the desert!

These pointy white teeth are actually snowdrifts! This plateau of Sur Lípez, Bolivia is found at 12,800 feet in altitude and has an extremely dry and cold climate (as low as -22 degrees Fahrenheit!). It's so cold that the snow hardens as it gets piled up by the wind. From June to August in the Southern Hemisphere, there are often snowfalls with winds reaching thirty-five miles per hour, creating these beautiful desert drifts.

BOLIVIA, SOUTH AMERICA

A city sculpted in the cliff!

Nearly twenty-five hundred years ago a nomadic desert tribe called the Nabataeans constructed this amazing city in the rosy sandstone cliffs. This city was named Petra, which means "rock" in Greek. Enclosed by the towering cliffs, Petra served as both a city and fortress. The Nabataeans carved palaces, temples, and splendid tombs out of the rock. Due to its magnificence, in 2007 Petra was named one of the new seven wonders of the world.

JORDAN, ASIA

crater Lake is located at an elevation of over six thousand feet!

Due to this lake's snow-covered shores and crystal blue water, you might think it is located in Antarctica or the North Pole, but it is actually in Oregon. Thousands of years ago an enormous volcano erupted and the resulting crater eventually became this lake. Crater Lake is 2,296 feet deep, making it the deepest lake in the United States and the seventh deepest in the world.

UNITED STATES, NORTH AMERICA

An army of 120 million red crabs has invaded the beach!

In the forests of Christmas Island, an Australian island in the Indian Ocean, live the Christmas Island red crabs, named for their very unusual bright red color. Every year the male crabs migrate to the ocean, where they are followed by the females. Mating and egg-laying both happen at the beach, where baby crabs hatch as larvae and swim into the ocean. After a month at sea, they return to shore and molt into mature, air-breathing land crabs. A year later, it happens all over again!

AUSTRALIA, OCEANIA

A slot canyon in colors!

Located in Arizona, this sandstone gorge is a true art gallery! A slot canyon is a narrow canyon that has been formed over time by the wear of water and wind. Fifty feet high and 1,312 feet long, this slot canyon is lit by rays of sunlight. The light rebounds on the sandstone walls and reflects a multitude of colors: gold, orange, red, gray, white, and purple.

UNITED STATES,
NORTH AMERICA

The fury of the sea is unleashed!

An enormous wave is about to sweep over the Jument lighthouse near the rocky coast of Brittany, at the westernmost tip of France. In this area, storms can be intense and last for several days. Fortunately, the lighthouse-keeper closed the door just in time to avoid being swept away—not the best time to peek outside! This lighthouse was built a century ago, in an area where strong currents have caused plenty of shipwrecks. Due to the rough surf, it took nine years to build!

FRANCE, EUROPE

water is not always blue!

Lake Natron is a saline (salty) lake in the Great Rift Valley of Tanzania. It is surrounded by volcanic mountains and fed by hot springs. The heat, saltiness, and mineral-laden water from the hot springs are the perfect breeding ground for the bacteria and algae that give the lake its fantastic red coloring. The lake is also a major home to flamingoes, who love to feast on its algae. An estimated 2.5 million flamingoes live in the valley!

TANZANIA, AFRICA

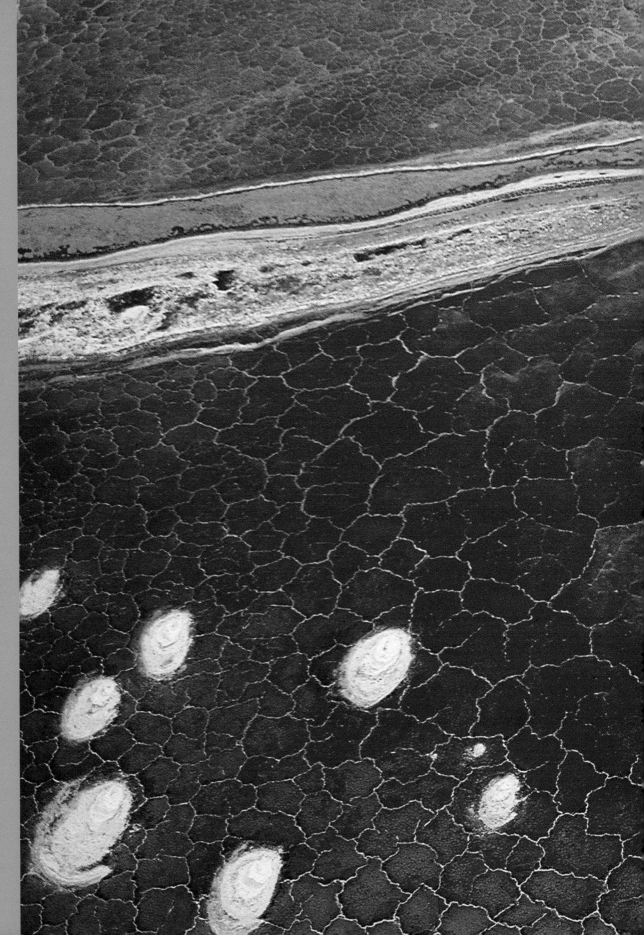

fountains in the middle of the desert.

Geysers are springs that occasionally spout hot water and steam—nature's fountains! The one shown here is called Fly Geyser. It is in a region of Nevada called Black Rock Desert, home to one of the largest flat surfaces on earth, a dry lake bed that covers over 11,000 square miles! The lake existed during the last ice age when the desert was covered with water.

UNITED STATES,
NORTH AMERICA

In Antarctica, blocks of ice change appearance every day.

Is it a running dog, a dinosaur walking on the water, or a jaguar in mid-stride? At the South Pole, the difference in daytime and nighttime temperatures cause many small fragments to splinter off the ice. This forces a constant reshaping of the ice, sometimes into surprising figures. Mother Nature continuously creates beautiful works of art!

ANTARCTICA

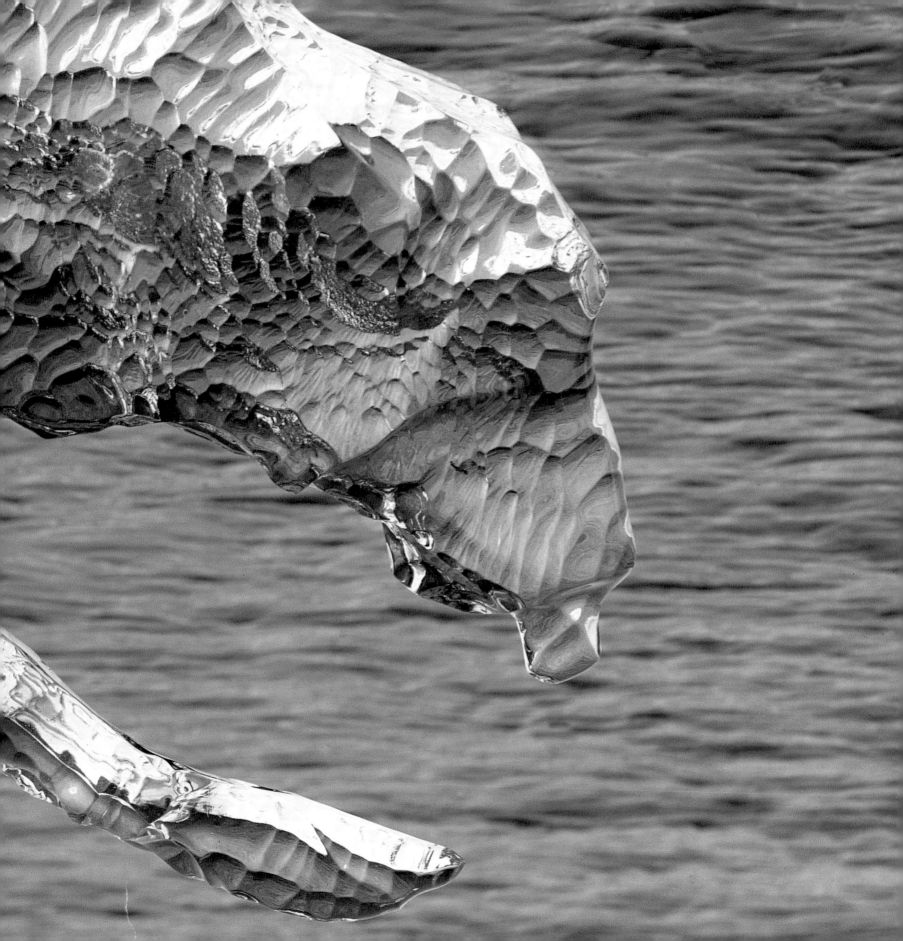

The Vermilion cliffs look like ice cream!

But don't be tempted to take a bite! These rocks of pink sandstone, stacked up like a giant swirl of ice cream, are found in the desert zones of Arizona. The thin yellow, orange, or red stripes that decorate them are due to the many minerals present in the earth. The colors shift and change depending on the available light and time of day.

UNITED STATES,
NORTH AMERICA

33

In canada, the Balanced Rocks keep their balance by themselves!

This natural curiosity defies the laws of physics! The column of stone has been eroded on each side, except on its small base, which supports the whole of the pillar. The rock is made of lava—dating from the age of the dinosaurs—that has hardened and been worn by the water. How does this rock keep its balance? It remains one of the mysteries of nature!

CANADA, NORTH AMERICA

35

The lava lake of Erta Ale, a bubbling cauldron!

This volcano in Ethiopia offers an amazing nighttime spectacle! The bright red and yellow colors reveal the presence of lava at the base of the well-shaped crater. It is one of the only active volcanoes in the world to have a permanent lake of lava. The crater's very fragile walls descend 295 feet straight down. Occasionally, when the lava is molten, the too-full crater overflows.

ETHIOPIA, AFRICA

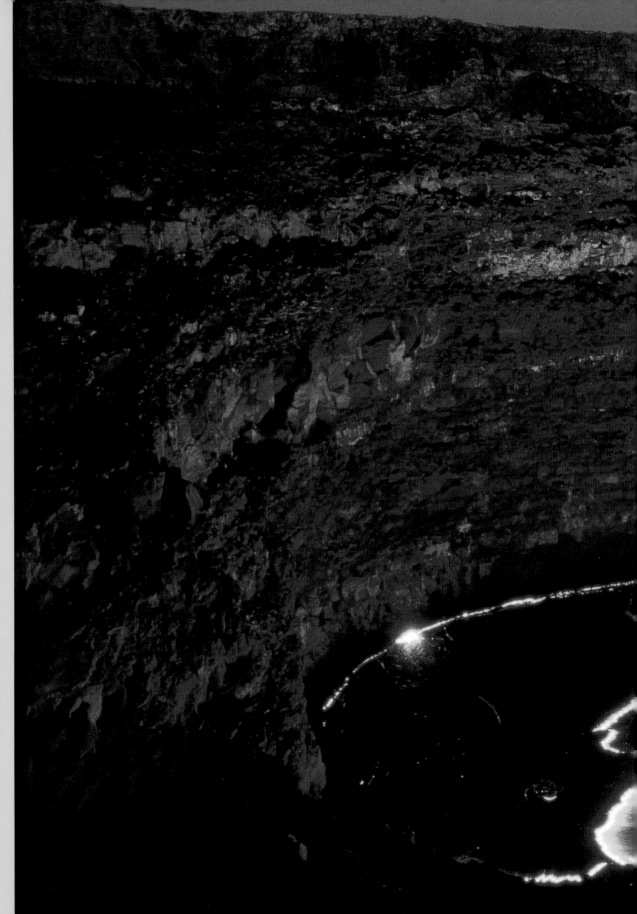

Rafflesia: the biggest flower in the world!

The flowers of the Rafflesia, also called the corpse flower, are gigantic. They can measure close to three feet in diameter (the width of a door) and weigh up to fifteen pounds! Those who get too close to the Rafflesia will not soon forget it: To attract insects for pollination, the flowers give off the strong odor of rotting meat! The Rafflesia has no stems and no leaves and survives by being a parasite to other plants.

MALAYSIA, ASIA

Melting icebergs form a fantastic variety of shapes!

This iceberg looks like a giant dining room table! Due to the movement of the sea and the steady increase in the temperature of the water, icebergs at the North Pole can break off from glaciers. Over time, the floating icebergs are hollowed out, taking unusual forms and becoming unbalanced. Eventually, the icebergs topple over on themselves and melt into the sea.

ARCTIC OCEAN

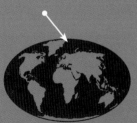

The Afar region, a lunar landscape.

Near the Red Sea, the Afar Triangle, from the name of a people in Ethiopia, is a very volcanic region. Thousands of stone formations, some of which reach more than 150 feet high, stand in this very arid land, the result of an evaporated sea. In certain places, it resembles the moon much more than the Earth!

ETHIOPIA, AFRICA

The bottom of the Red Sea, a floor of fluorescent-colored coral!

Although these little colored branches look like flowers, they are coral: marine animals that live in colonies. Coral has a soft skeleton and tentacles that serve as shelter for numerous schools of fish. At night, the tentacles unfurl and capture microscopic animals, plants, and plankton. These vibrant colors come from an algae called *zooxanthella,* which supplies coral with essential nutrients (and beautiful colors) and, in return, gets a protective home.

RED SEA, AFRICA

In Australia, the Remarkable Rocks look like strange beasts!

Vulture heads, gigantic fangs, skulls, fantastic animals . . . The rocks on Kangaroo Island, South Australia, were transformed into many imaginative shapes by the movement of the swirling wind and sea, and can reach the height of a three-story building. These oddly formed blocks of granite are well-named the Remarkable Rocks.

AUSTRALIA, OCEANIA

47

Summer or winter, the temperature of the Blue Lagoon's water is 104 degrees Fahrenheit.

This peculiar scene can be found in Iceland. Under the ground, numerous springs are heated by molten volcanic rock; one spring feeds into the geothermal power plant in the background. The extra water from the power station is released into this artificial lake, called the Blue Lagoon. Due to the water's mix of minerals, silica, and even algae, many people bathe in the water for its reputed healing qualities.

ICELAND, EUROPE

Grand Prismatic Spring, a giant pool of hot water.

Seen from the sky, this expanse of water seems so big that the people on the walkway look like ants! In fact, this hot spring discharges more than 4,050 gallons of boiling water per minute. Microscopic algae (microorganisms called hyperthermophiles) create these magnificent colors, which change according to the temperature of the water. Situated in Yellowstone National Park, it's the largest hot spring in the United States.

UNITED STATES, NORTH AMERICA

51

Glacier caves: shafts that are deep and blue... and completely made of ice!

When any part of a glacier's ice melts, the resulting water flows along the surface of the glacier. This causes streams at the top of the glacier that can vary in size from a simple trickle to a veritable river. The water flows downward to the interior of the glacier through tubular holes in the glacier called moulin. The moulin can become very wide and deep if the glacier's melting is sizeable, creating these stunning caves of ice.

GREENLAND, NORTH AMERICA

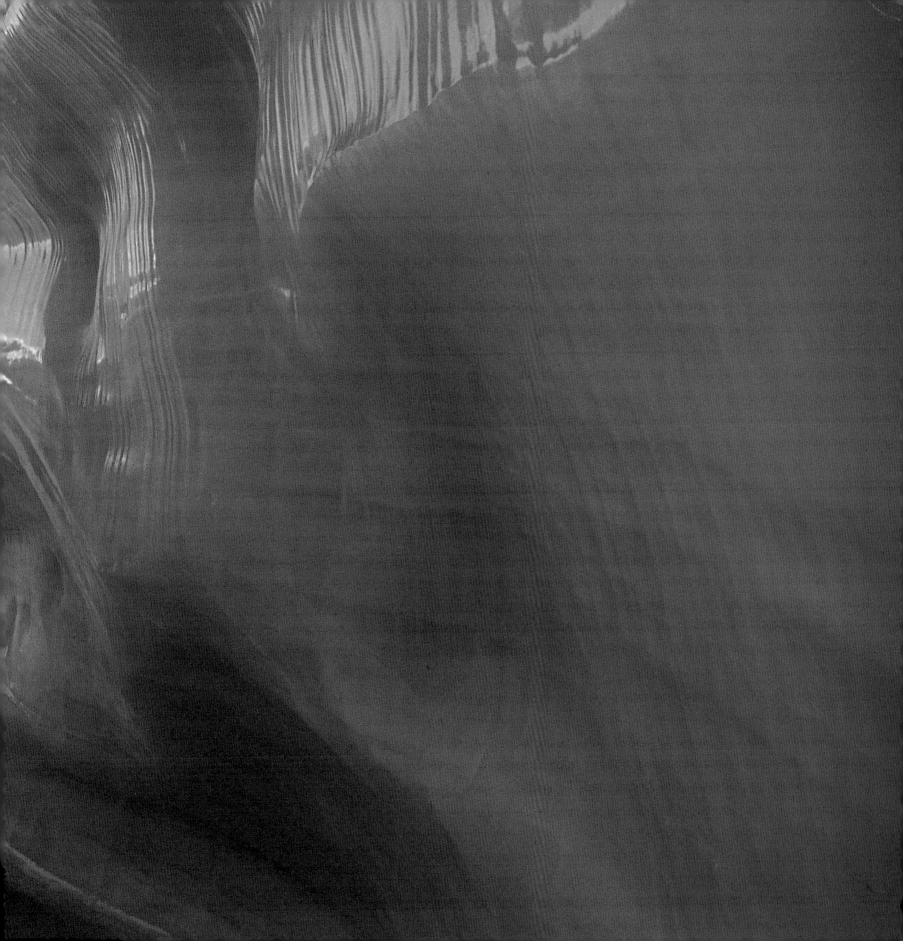

This crater is the imprint of a meteorite.

Most meteors that travel through space self-destruct when they enter the Earth's atmosphere. However, every once in a while, one of them lands on our planet! The proof: Meteor Crater in the Arizona desert. It was formed by the fall of a large meteorite about fifty thousand years ago. Judging by the crater's size it must have been huge: The impact measures 4,000 feet in diameter and 570 feet in depth!

UNITED STATES, NORTH AMERICA

This tree is the oldest on the planet.

The Great Basin bristlecone pine holds the record for longevity among trees. The one seen here, rooted in a dry mountainous region of California, is getting ready to celebrate its 4,770th birthday! Like wrinkles on skin, crevasses line its trunk. In its younger years, its bark was smooth and gray. But don't go looking for it—the exact location of the oldest bristlecone pine is kept a strict secret so that it can age in peace!

UNITED STATES,
NORTH AMERICA

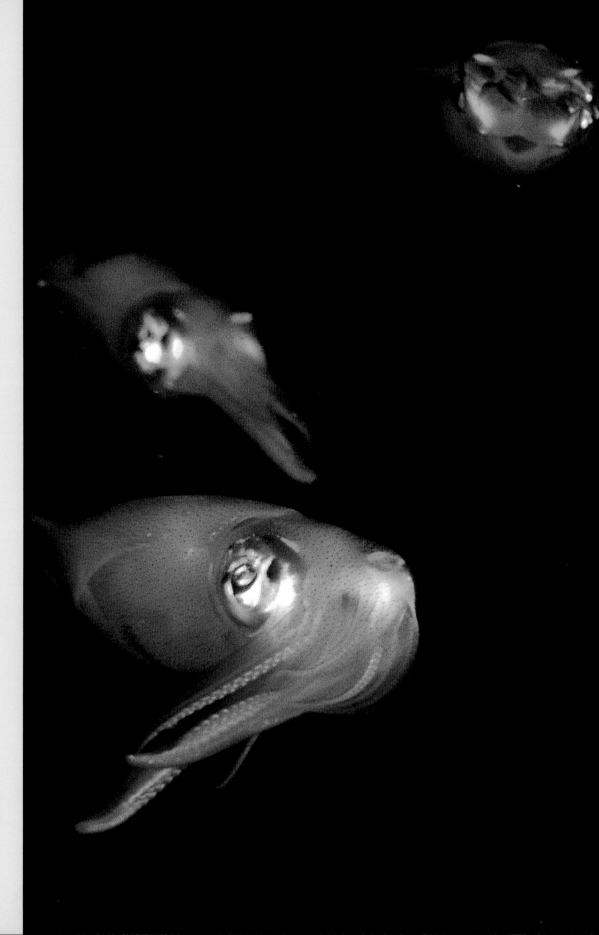

These Squid glow deep in the Pacific Ocean.

These squid are bioluminescent, which means they are able to emit light. Some types of squid use this feature when they are threatened by a predator; the sudden flash distracts and startles the enemy, so that the squid can get away! Some squid use their "glow" to attract mates and find members of their own species. This is particularly helpful when swimming in the dark, lower regions of the ocean.

INDONESIA, ASIA

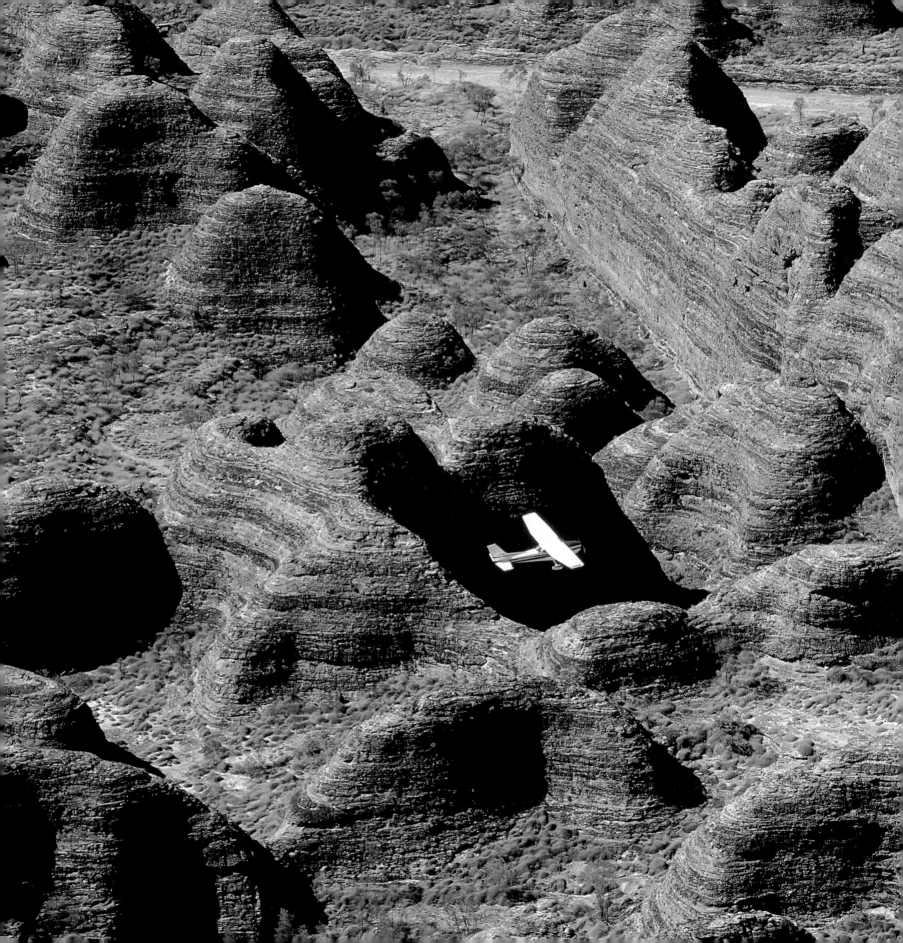

The Bungle Bungle Range: funny hills with a funny name!

In rural western Australia, nature has modeled mountains in curves and dressed them with black and orange stripes. Their rounded forms result from the slow work of erosion, and the "tiger-like" coloring comes from the composition of the sandy rock, made of lichen (black) and of silica and iron (orange). But the Bungle Bungle Range is almost as fragile as a sand castle. Hikers may admire them, but are not permitted to climb them.

AUSTRALIA, OCEANIA

The rocks of the White Desert look like limestone meringues!

These surprising rock formations can be found in the middle of one of the most beautiful deserts in Egypt. They are the result of a mysterious sculptor: wind loaded with sand! Over time, thousands of these rocks, many as high as a two-story building, have been eroded to create a landscape that appears to be truly magical. When the sun sets, these chalky rocks seem to glow!

EGYPT, AFRICA

63

A real-life magical forest!

In the Rwenzori Mountains of Uganda (situated on the equator) lots of light, humidity, and highly fluctuating temperatures work together to create some very amazing plants. These funny plants, called giant groundsels, can grow up to thirty feet tall. During the chilly nights, they close their cabbage-like tops to protect against frost. Oddly enough, these giants are in the same plant family as daisies and dandelions!

UGANDA, AFRICA

The Perito Moreno Glacier is on the move!

Over eighteen miles long and three miles wide, this glacier is located in Los Glaciares National Park in Patagonia, Argentina. This wall of ice is advancing by over two thousand feet per year! The movement creates enormous pressure in the ice, and very powerful cracking noises. The denser and more packed the ice is, the bluer the color. It's so tall (two hundred feet) that when a several-ton block of ice falls from the top, it causes gigantic waves in Lago Argentina.

ARGENTINA, SOUTH AMERICA

In tropical forests, certain trees have roots that look like ribbons!

Buttressed tree trunks—those with woody, supportive extensions—are found in many tropical rain forests. When trees are growing in areas with soil that is poor in nutrients, these roots help to get the food and water they need to live. The roots can grow fifteen feet above the soil and expand horizontally, to cover the widest area possible in order to collect nourishment—a big advantage in shallow soil.

AUSTRALIA, OCEANIA

68

Pretty but dangerous: It is impossible to swim in Lake Voui!

Approximately 425 years ago, the Lombenben volcano on Aoba Island (also called Ambae Island) exploded, creating this crater lake with its beautiful turquoise water. However, due to volcanic activity, this is a lake unlike any other: Its water is so hot and acidic that it would eat away the skin of your finger if you dipped it in! Only researchers and scientists risk navigating the lake in order to study it.

VANUATU ARCHIPELAGO, OCEANIA

Goblin Valley, a mysterious and amazing landscape...

These mushroom-shaped formations, a few feet high, resemble little goblins wearing big hats. Thousands of these geological oddballs are located in Utah's Goblin Valley State Park. In this desert region, the wind (loaded with sand), extreme temperatures, and water runoff have created this forest of strange creatures!

UNITED STATES, NORTH AMERICA

walls of water: a mighty force of nature!

The size of a wave depends on the force of the wind, its duration, and the amount of surface water over which it blows. When the curve of the wave is very significant, it breaks on the shore, producing a white foam froth. Certain waves, called tidal waves or tsunamis, are caused by an underwater earthquake. These tsunamis can move under the water at more than 425 miles per hour (two times faster than a Formula One race car!) and ravage everything in their path.

PACIFIC OCEAN, NORTH AMERICA

water and wind are talented sculptors!

Over time, wind, rain, and frost can wear down rock: splintering it into fragments, corroding it, hollowing out holes, or polishing it. Sometimes, strange forms are born of this slow work, like this balanced rock in Texas, which looks like a giant pebble wedged between two rocks. This natural rock formation creates a "window" onto scenic Big Bend National Park.

UNITED STATES, NORTH AMERICA

77

The jungle weaves its roots around the temples of Angkor Wat.

These amazing temples were constructed in Angkor, Cambodia during the twelfth century. Some of these temples, long abandoned, have been overrun by banyan trees, giants of the tropical forest. Over time, the roots of the banyans have squeezed between the temples' stones, covering or lifting them up. But today these man-made buildings and Mother Nature support each other. Without the trees, the walls would collapse, and without the walls, the trees could no longer stand upright!

CAMBODIA, ASIA

The JOSHUA tree, a giant hedgehog in the desert!

Able to grow up to nearly twenty feet high, the Joshua tree possesses long branches covered with very prickly leaves that protect its fruit. It's one tough tree: It can withstand long dry periods, its seeds can wait for many years in the ground for rain to germinate them, and its bark even resists fire very well. It grows in the Mojave Desert, not far from Death Valley, California.

UNITED STATES, NORTH AMERICA

The salt pans of Maras have existed since the twelfth century.

In Peru, the salt pans of Maras form a patchwork of four thousand white pools clinging to the side of a mountain in the Andes. From above, the locals channel saltwater that bubbles from a hot spring into a network of canals. These canals carry the water to each pool. Under the heat of the sun, the water evaporates and leaves behind crystals of salt, which can then be harvested. This system, created in the Middle Ages by pre-Columbian people, is still used today.

PERU, SOUTH AMERICA

A shower of lightning bolts!

These lightning flashes, often accompanied by claps of thunder, correspond to a discharge of electricity, either between the ground and a cloud or between two clouds. While lightning usually measures about a mile long, the longest recorded lightning bolt was 118 miles long! Lightning is also fast, traveling at an unimaginable speed of 136,000 miles per hour. On average, there are one hundred lightning flashes per second throughout the world!

UNITED STATES,
NORTH AMERICA

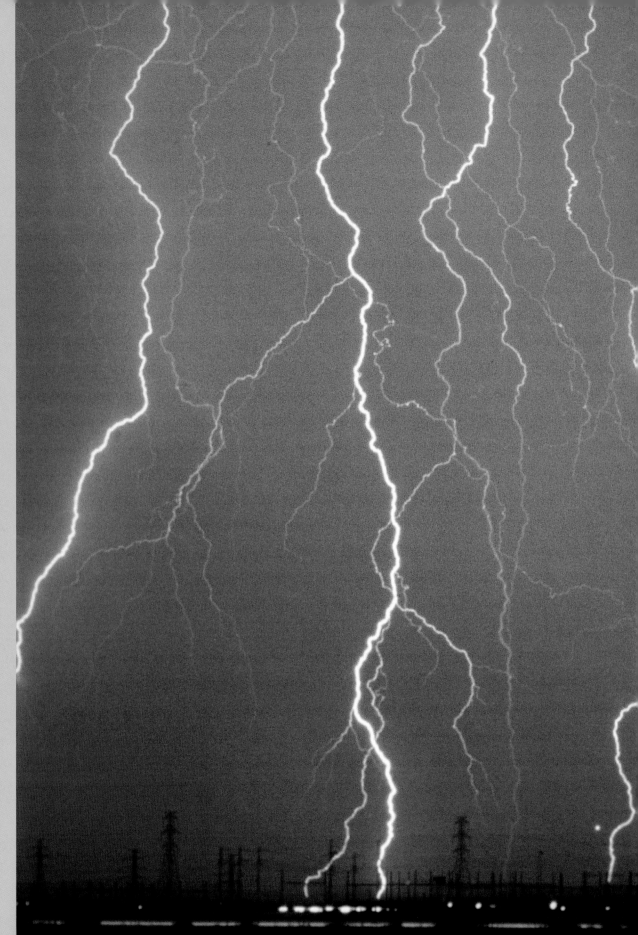

Shibam, the city with the oldest skyscrapers.

In the middle of the desert in Yemen stands this very unique city. Its oldest buildings, constructed twenty-five hundred years ago, possess exceptional architecture for that time. From five to seven stories tall, they look like skyscrapers from a distance, but are actually made up of stone and mud—not steel and concrete, like buildings today. Shibam is called "Manhattan of the desert!"

YEMEN, ASIA

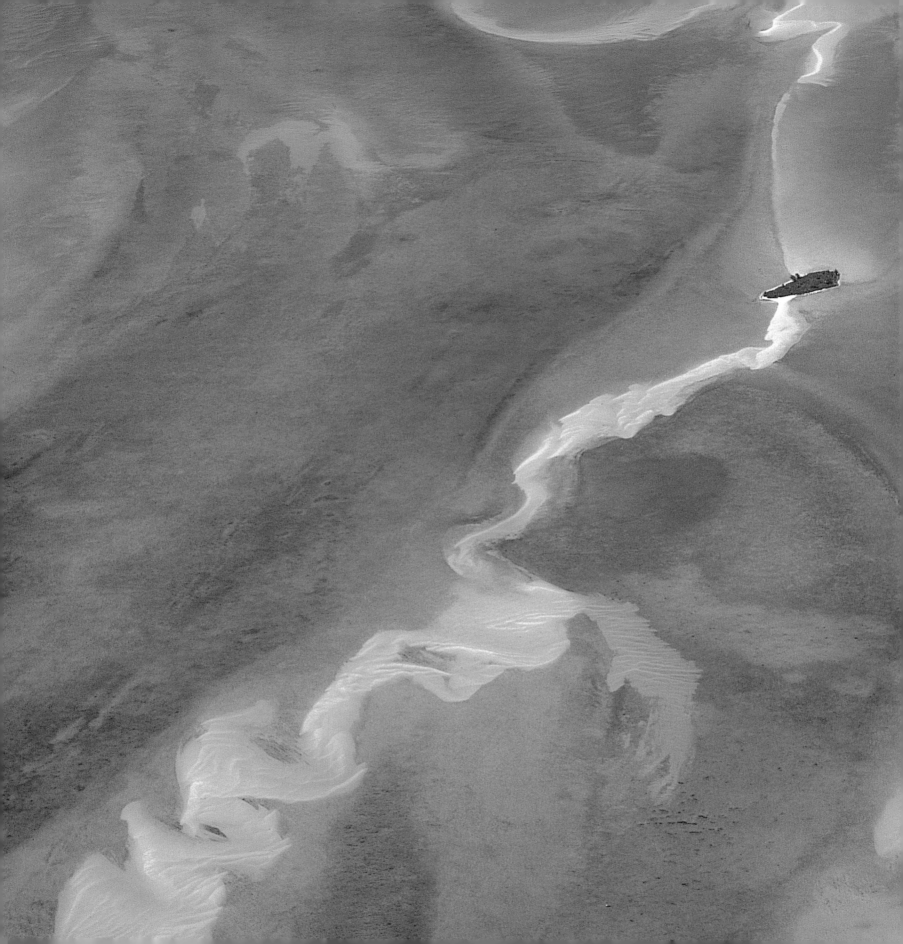

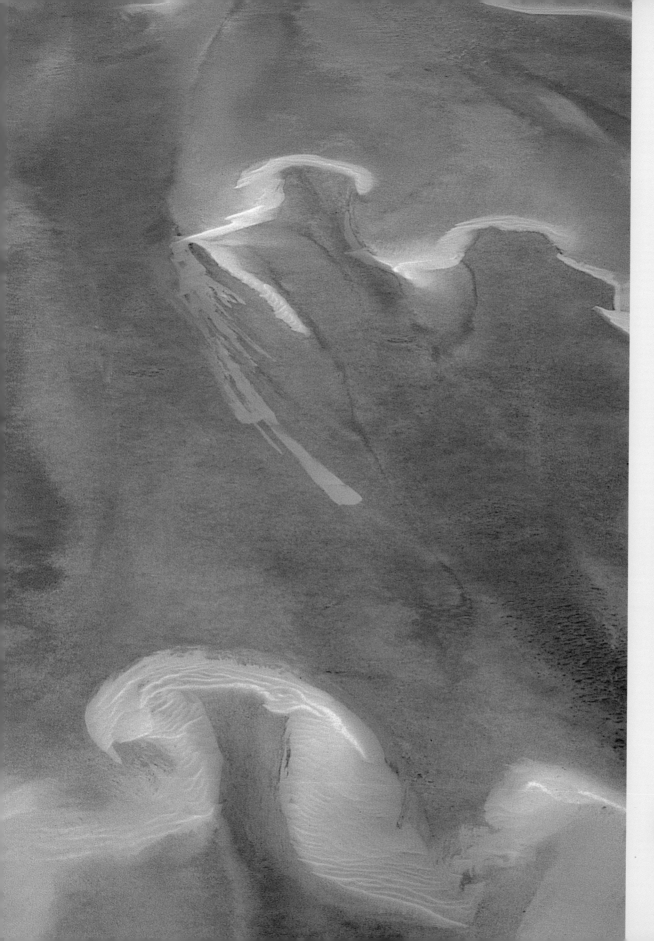

An island alone in the middle of the Atlantic Ocean.

The Bahamas, in the Caribbean Sea, are made up of hundreds of tiny islands. This region of coral barrier reefs and very long sandbanks could almost be crossed on foot because the water is not very deep, except for certain places called "blue holes." Seven hundred islands and twenty-five hundred islets (tiny islands) form this 745-mile-long archipelago, of which only twenty are permanently inhabited.

BAHAMAS, NORTH AMERICA

89

In Ethiopia, hot springs make rocks ooze!

These hills, overflowing with yellow, white, and green liquids, are hot springs: a result of volcanic activity in the Danakil region. The limestone content of the water dissolves at high temperatures and bubbles back up to the surface, forming peaks thirty to sixty feet high that trickle steaming, hot water. The vivid colors are due to the presence of bacteria that develops and grows in the heated water.

ETHIOPIA, AFRICA

Biking through... Death Valley!

Bicycling in Death Valley, one of the hottest places on the planet: what a challenge! This big, very steep-sided valley in California is the lowest point in America, at 282 feet *below* sea level. Because it is isolated from the wind and clouds by surrounding mountains, it posts an average temperature of 113 degrees Fahrenheit! Tourists are advised to bring plenty of water with them and to stay very close to the paved road.

UNITED STATES,
NORTH AMERICA

Index

Special Thanks to:

Christopher Hardin, Jennifer Vetter, Cheryl Weisman, L. Maj, L. Bouton, B. Legendre, C. Boulud, F. Michaud, A. Pichlak, John Candell, and Paula Manzanero

Photography credits

BIOS
30-31: J.M. Bour. 32-33: F. Suchel. 80-81: P. Arnold/Wilstie.
CORBIS
4-5: A. Garcia. 24-25: J. Guichard. 28-29: S.T. Smith. 66-67: T. Allofs. 76-77: P. A. Souders. 78-79: T. Bognar. 82-83: H. Stadler.
COSMOS
48-49, 88-89: B. Edmaier/SPL. 50-51: P. Steinmetz. 74-75: R. Brown. 84-85: W. Faidley/International Stock.
EXPLORER
16-17: E. Sampers.
GETTY IMAGES
10-11: P. Wakefield. 46-47: R. Smith.
O. GRUNEWALD
8-9, 36-37, 72-73, 90-91.
HEMISPHERE
34-35: C. Heeb.
HOA-QUI
2: P. De Wilde. 6-7: C. Vaisse. 26-27, 52-53, 64-65, 70-71: Ph. Bourseiller. 42-43: Bourseiller/Durieux. 62-63: C. Sappa.
JACANA
12-13: J. Freund. 38-39: Jouan/Rius. 56-57: J. Foott/NPL.
PHO.N.E.
14-15: C. Jardel. 18-19: F. Gohier. 20-21: J.-P. Ferrero. 44-45: D. Brandelet. 60-61: Ferroro/Auscape.
PHOTONONSTOP
86-87: C. Marshal. 92-93: G. Simeone.
SUNSET
22-23: J. Warden. 40-41: F.L.P.A. 68-69: Photo Ant.

ISBN-13: 978-1-60214-058-5

Play Bac Publishing USA, Inc.
225 Varick Street
New York, NY 10014-4381

infospbusa@playbac.fr
Contact number : +12126147725

Printed in Singapore

Distributed by Black Dog & Leventhal Publishers, Inc.
151 West 19th Street
New York, NY 10011

First Printing, October 2008

April/2009